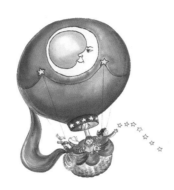

THE
MOON BALLOON

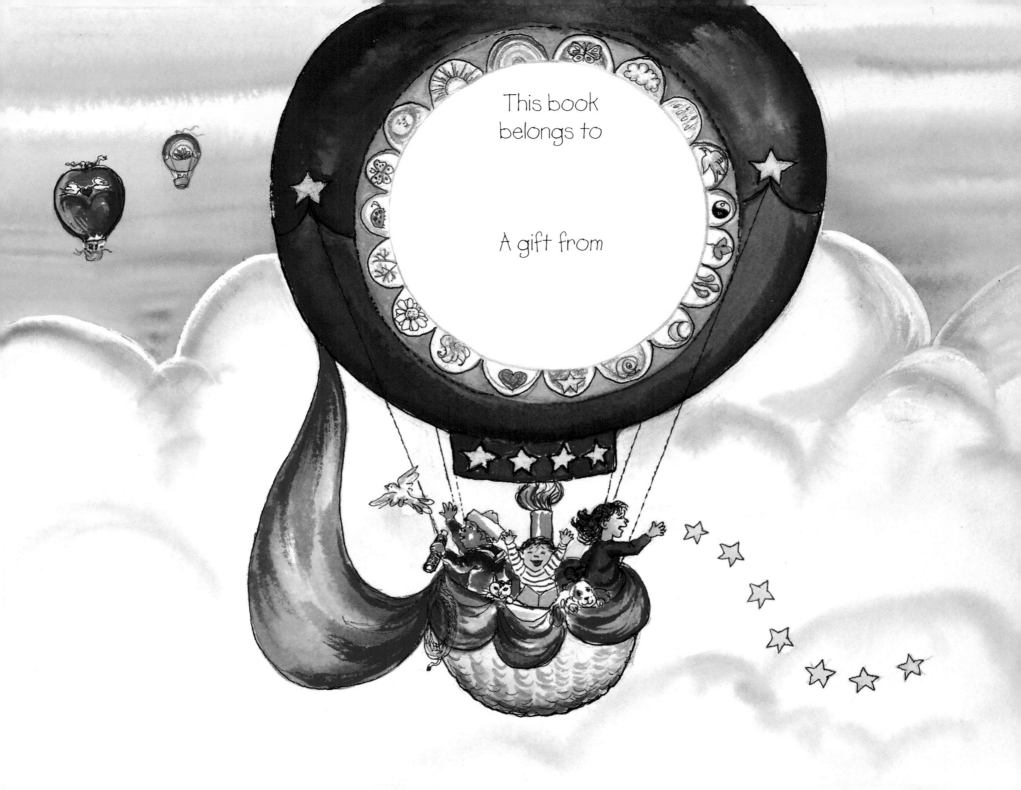

This book
belongs to

A gift from

New Revised Edition of the Beloved Classic

THE
MOON
BALLOON

A Journey
of Hope and Discovery
for Children and Families

by

Joan Drescher

Foreword by Joan Borysenko, Ph.D.

Published by The Moon Balloon Project, Inc.

FOREWORD

The Moon Balloon is a very special gift, taking children and all those who love and care for them on a remarkable journey of healing. This wonderful resource combines the opportunity for children to create their own stories of hope and discovery, enticed by the wonder and magic of hot air balloons and other colorful and playful artistic symbols.

Through this book, author/artist Joan Drescher engages children in the understanding of healing as an emotional-spiritual process that deeply affects their relationships—to themselves and others. *The Moon Balloon* is a wonderful way of allowing children to access and give words to their emotions.

My academic and personal fascination with the power of the mind to heal led to an exploration of the role of imagination in healing when I was an instructor in Medicine at Harvard Medical School and Director of a Mind/Body Clinic at one of the Harvard teaching hospitals. I have come to understand that healing is different from curing. Curing is a physical process aimed at eliminating disease. Healing is an emotional-spiritual process that deeply affects the relationship between self and other. Healing stimulates the body's reparative processes and it can increase the possibility that medical intervention will lead to a cure.

Relationships are the essence of healing. Research has shown time and time again that people who experience illness or trauma have better immune function, less distress, an enhanced quality of life and a

greater chance of cure when they can give voice to their emotions. Sometimes people, both adults and children, are mistakenly encouraged to deny their fears in the hope of easing their minds. But in fact, we feel better when strong feelings are expressed, heard and acknowledged. Only then, when the dark clouds of unexpressed emotion have parted, can hope and love be honestly expressed.

The visual elements of this book have already been used to help children in a variety of settings express their emotions and feel better about themselves and the world around them. Joan has been using the Moon Balloon workshops in hospitals, hospices and a variety of other settings both here and abroad for the last twenty years. Medical professionals, teachers and parents have found this book to be an essential tool in helping children to communicate their feelings. Children everywhere are opening these pages and climbing into a window of hope and possibility. Today adults can also experience the power of symbols through the new edition of *On Wings of Light, Finding Hope When the Heart Needs Healing,* which I co-created with Joan Drescher.

Please use *The Moon Balloon* with courage, joy, and reverence for the many insights, revelations and holy moments that it will surely help bring about. Climb into a balloon—and Godspeed on your journey.

—Joan Borysenko, Ph.D.
Author of *Minding the Body, Mending the Mind*

A NOTE TO PARENTS & OTHER CAREGIVERS

"The Moon Balloon is more than a storybook for my four-year-old daughter, Molly. When we first read the book together, the wonderful colors and shapes of the images inspired her to create five expressive drawings." —David Moir, Parent

The Moon Balloon provides a safe, supportive outlet to help children cope with the stress and mixed up feelings that often accompany illness, change, or any new situation. By experiencing this book, children gain the reassurance and support needed to develop a positive self-image and a healthy sense of self-esteem. You can use *The Moon Balloon* as a picture book with very young children or as a drawing and verbal exercise for older children. Whatever the age, *The Moon Balloon* offers a way that children can write and draw about dreams or anxieties that they often can't talk about. A child going through a difficult time can find comfort and encouragement in repeating the affirmations (marked with a small star) with you.

The Moon Balloon can be used by children individually or in groups. Guides can be parents, teachers, therapists, nurses, physicians, or anyone who cares about helping children express their feelings.

Your role as a guide is to encourage exploration of a child's inner world in a safe and positive way. It is important to maintain a comfortable sense of pacing as you go through the book. Let the child set the pace—only go as far as the child wants to go at any one time. This keeps the changes positive and progressive, and also encourages the children's growing sense of confidence and control. They key is to be supportive of whatever emotions are expressed. There are no "right or wrong answers." It is also important to be aware that children may or may not want to share their feelings with you or others. Respect the child's wishes. In all cases, please be patient, this can be a special journey of growth for both you and the child.

"I feel like I'm flying on my skateboard when I read The Moon Balloon."
—Alex Rovello, Age 11

Some helpful hints:

• Although all artwork is copywritten in the name of Joan Drescher, she gives users permission to photocopy the black and white pages for non-commercial educational uses only. In this way, the pages of the Moon Balloon book can be used again and again by the same child, or shared in a classroom setting. Have crayons or markers and pencils handy for the child to use to color and write on the photocopied pages.

• Create a quiet, comfortable environment where you will not be interrupted. You might even play soft music and set the stage by suggesting that the child or group of children imagine taking off in a hot air balloon. To introduce the book and help the imagination process begin, read together the "Note to Kids." Very young children can participate by pointing to the "read along" pictures. You may then want to read the entire book out loud.

• After reading the book, revisit each balloon in the Field of Balloon, encouraging the child or group of children to share feelings about each balloon.

• Always be supportive and accepting. Remember, there are no "right" answers. Respect the child's emotions, even if they are unpleasant. Some children may prefer to keep this book as a personal journey and not share it with anyone. This is okay. Provide a private place for the book's safekeeping.

• For more information about working with kids as they explore *The Moon Balloon*, read in the back of this book about author Joan Drescher. For resources on workshops, activities, the user's guide, and the Moon Balloon Project, Inc., visit our website, www.themoonballoon.com.

A NOTE TO KIDS

The Balloon is a special book for you to use and enjoy. It will take you on a trip in an air balloon! During your trip you will get in touch with the most powerful gift you have, your own imagination.

When you're unhappy you often forget the joy in life. Maybe you have to stay in bed when you wish you were out playing with other kids!

IT'S NOT FAIR!

You might feel alone, sad, helpless, happy and angry all at the same time. These feelings are o.k. It is natural to feel them.

Using your imagination The Balloon will take you to the Field of Balloons where each balloon you visit is a feeling you might have. Have fun with them by writing and drawing your feelings on each balloon.

It is [o.k.] to make extra ☀ photocopies of the black and white pages, so you can write in it again and again. Sharing the book with others can be wonderful, 🖤 but if you want to keep it private 🗝 that's [o.k.,] too. This is your book.

Have fun!

I hope The 🌙 Balloon will (comfort) you when you are feeling ☹ down, give you giggles 😀 😀 😀 as well as ⭐ ⭐ courage ⭐ and help you get in touch with your own ✨ powerful ✨ magic…

(your imagination.)

But most of all, I hope The 🌙 Balloon will become your friend.

🖤 🖤 Love 🖤 🖤

Joan Drescher

7

The Moon Balloon
is waiting to take you
on a journey
to your favorite place.

So climb in the basket.
You may bring a friend
or a pet.

In the bottom of the basket
you will find a slip of paper
with flight instructions.

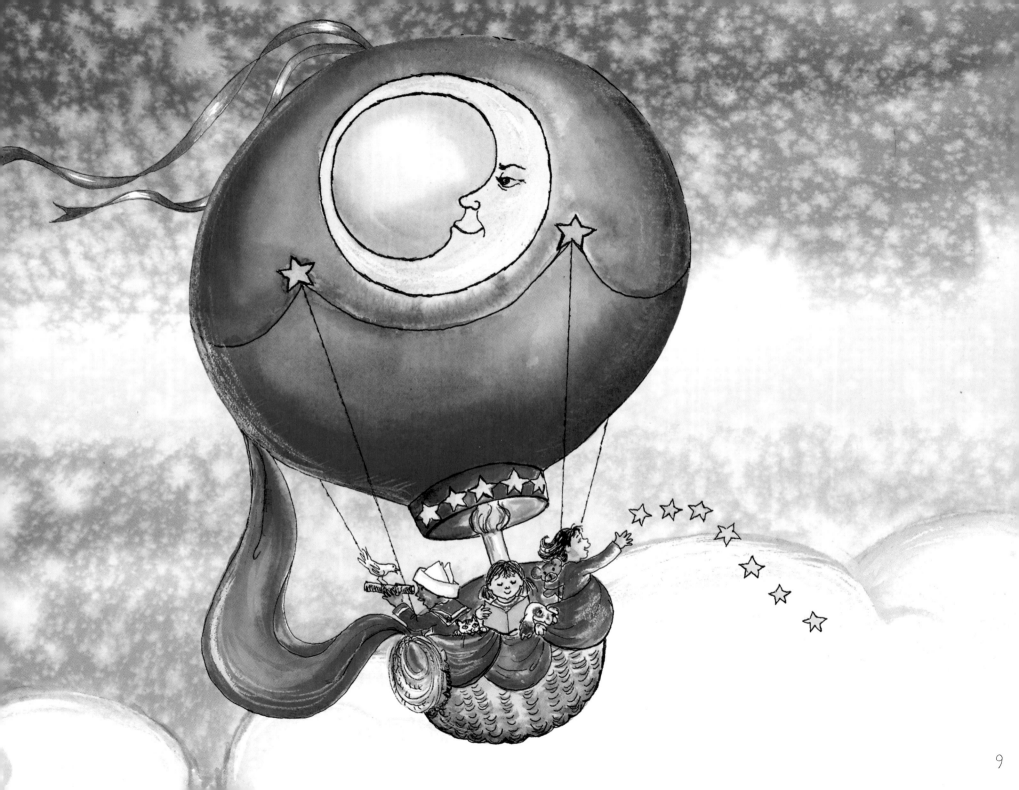

INSTRUCTIONS FOR TAKE OFF

1. Take a deep breath and let it out.

2. Use the fire in the Air Balloon to spark your imagination.

3. Every balloon has a sandbag full of heavy things like fear, worry and anxiety.

4. In order to go up, you need to be light. So let go of the sandbags one by one.

5. Drop fear, worry and anxious feelings out with the sand.

6. When you are done you will feel very light and your balloon will begin to go up.

7. In the bottom of the basket are seven stars. As you begin to rise, send each star to someone you love.

You can name each star

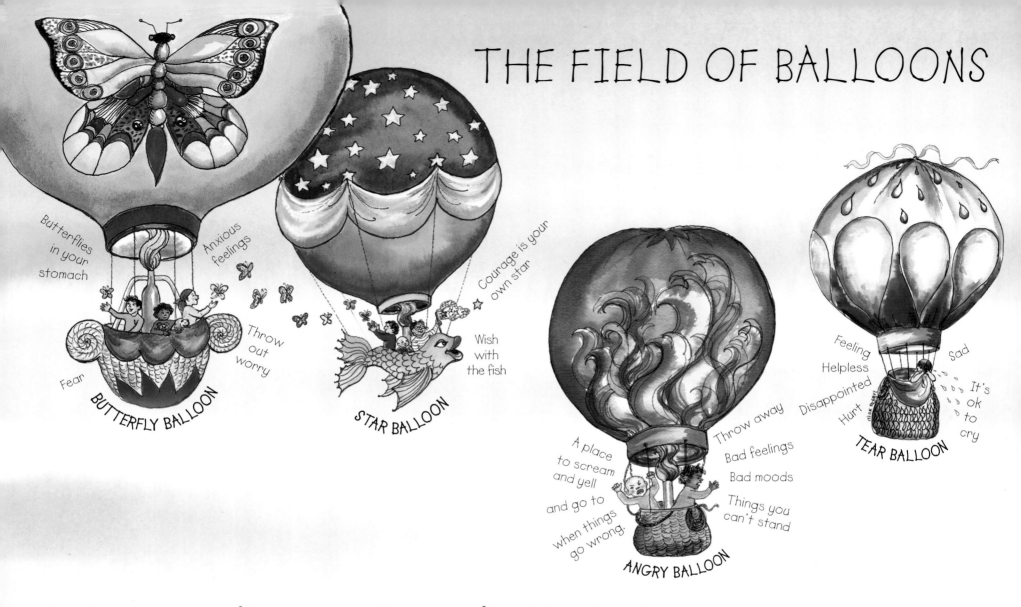

Butterflies in your stomach

Anxious feelings

Fear

Throw out worry

BUTTERFLY BALLOON

Courage is your own star

Wish with the fish

STAR BALLOON

A place to scream and yell and go to when things go wrong.

Throw away

Bad feelings

Bad moods

Things you can't stand

ANGRY BALLOON

Feeling Helpless

Disappointed

Hurt

Sad

It's ok to cry

TEAR BALLOON

During your flight you will see soft white clouds passing by you. The wind sings a song in your ears.

Soon you will come to a place in the sky where you see tiny bits of color. As you get closer you see it is the Field of Balloons.

SUN BALLOON

Peace
Beauty
Summer days
Warm feelings

PEACE BALLOON

Feeling Safe
Welcome
Resting quietly
Sweet dreams
Wind songs

GIGGLE BALLOON

Joy
Laughter
Giggles
Smiles
Fun

Jokes
Ha-Ha
Ho-Ho
Tee-Hee
Fun

LOVE BALLOON

Open your heart
Give to others
Be kind

Miracles
Wonder
Hugs
Magic
Joy

STRESS BALLOON

FAST
CONFLICT
NOISE
TOO MUCH
TOO MANY
THINGS
WINNING AND LOSING
TIME RUNNING OUT
POLLUTION

No time for me
Bad TV news

Too much
Too fast
Too loud
Too many things to do

Each balloon is a feeling you might have.
Sometimes we have more than one feeling. All of these feelings are o.k.

You can choose to visit whichever balloon you like, depending on
how you feel. Visit them again and again whenever you like!

13

If you are feeling scared or have butterflies in your stomach,
climb into the Butterfly Balloon and throw them out.
The Star Balloon will surely catch them.

The Star Balloon has a fish for a basket. Make a wish with the fish in the
Star Balloon. He will give you a special star to give you courage.

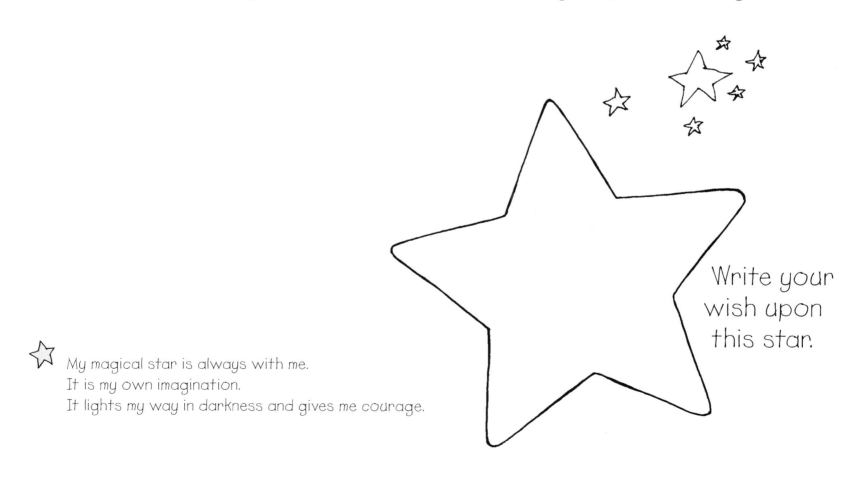

Write your
wish upon
this star.

My magical star is always with me.
It is my own imagination.
It lights my way in darkness and gives me courage.

The Sun Balloon will warm you and comfort you. Its bright sunshine fills you with beauty and warmth. It will take you to the Land of Summer Days where you can hear birds singing, smell wild flowers and feel the warmth of the sun on your back.

☆ I see the light of the sun.
I feel warmth.
I feel safe.

16

SUMMER TREASURES

Draw a picture of your favorite summer day.
Fill the basket with treasures you found on the beach,
in the grass or just anywhere.

The Stress Balloon is
a place to go
   when everything seems
   like too much!
   You can leave a lot
   of things that
   are driving you crazy
in this balloon.

 Sometimes I feel so stressed that I'm ready to explode!
Before I pop, I visit the Stress Balloon.

When you are finished
take a deep breath
and get ready to leave.
The Peace Balloon
is waiting for you!

Throw everything
that makes you feel
stressed into the basket

Write and draw how you feel here.

2 MUCH 2 FAST
NO TIME FOR ME
2 MANY THINGS TO DO
BUZZ

The Peace Balloon
is a safe quiet place.
The wind rocks you gently
and sings you a lullaby.
Your balloon rises slowly
into the clouds. Relax,
you don't have to do
anything here.
Just be yourself.

I rest quietly and visit the peaceful place inside of me.
I feel welcome and safe. I can visit this place whenever I like.

Close your eyes and take a deep breath.
Let your mind go to the peaceful place inside of you.

Put your favorite dreams in the basket.

Pick a cloud. Write down a dream. Remember your dreams are always here waiting for you!

The Tear Balloon
is for catching your tears.
It is all right to feel
sad and cry when
you're in the Tear Balloon.

Fill the basket full of pain,
disappointment, sadness
and hurtful feelings.

☆ I give myself permission to feel my saddest feelings.
It's o.k. for me to cry.

You can write or draw
what makes you feel
sad and put it in the
empty basket of
the Tear Balloon.

You can also draw
yourself when you
feel sad or alone,
or just fill the
basket with tears.

It is very deep!

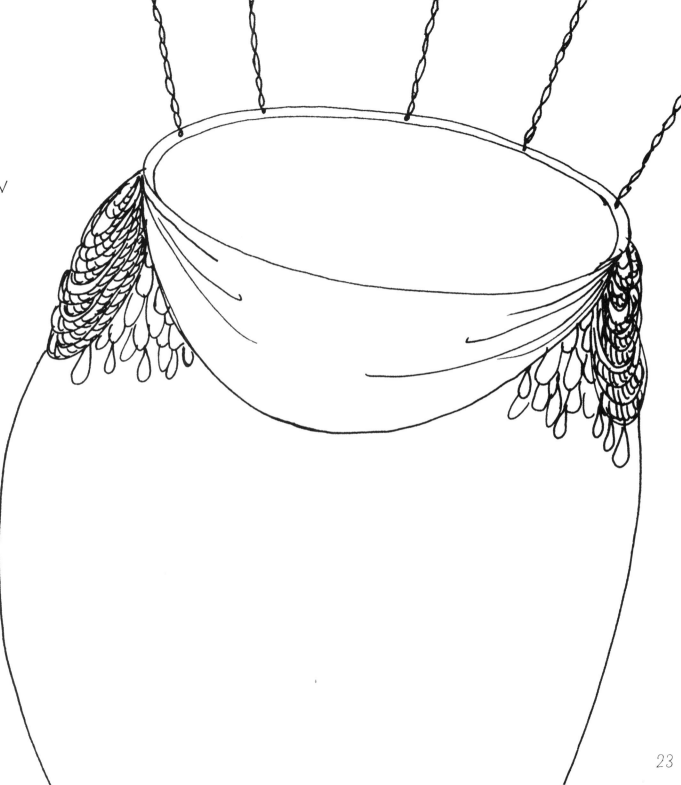

The Angry Balloon
is the place to go
when you're feeling
really mad or upset.
You can put all the
things that make you mad
in this balloon.
It is a place to let go
of bad feelings.

Sometimes
when things go wrong
we think it is our fault.

It is not your fault.

☆ It is o.k. to be angry.

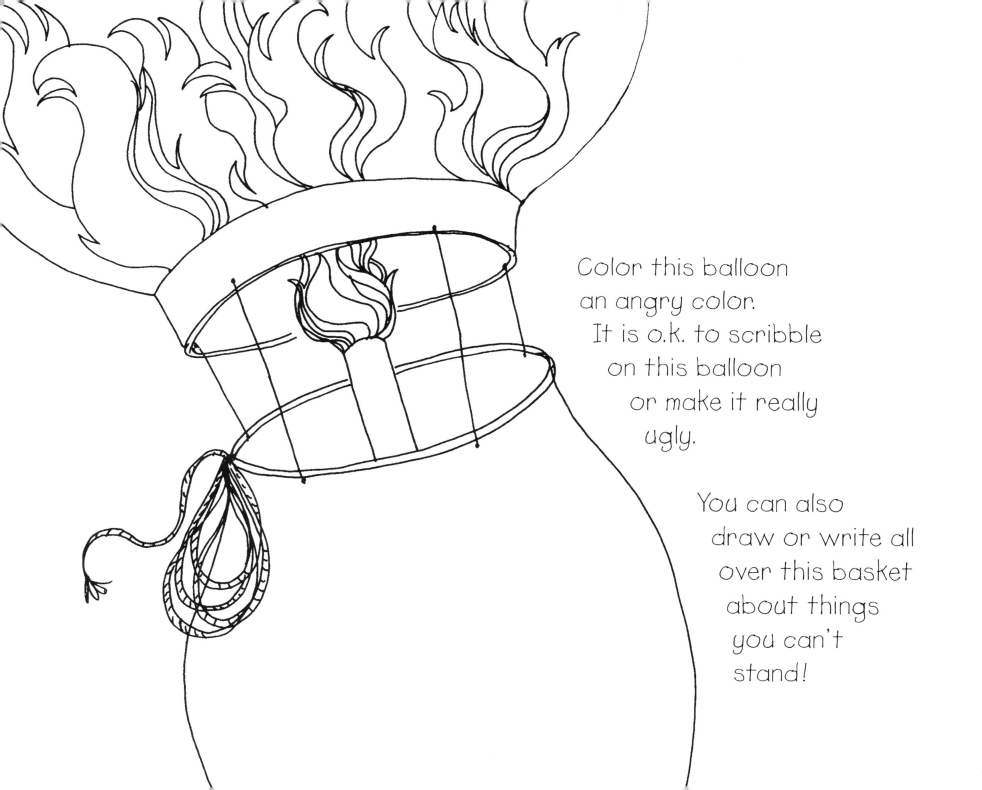

Color this balloon
an angry color.
It is o.k. to scribble
on this balloon
or make it really
ugly.

You can also
draw or write all
over this basket
about things
you can't
stand!

Tickle your toes
and make a funny face.

The Giggle Balloon
will take you to
the laughing place.

Close your eyes and turn
the corners of your mouth up
into a smile. Let the smile go into a giggle.

As you giggle your balloon goes higher
and higher up into the clouds, where
you laugh out loud with the birds in the sky!

The more you laugh, the higher you go...

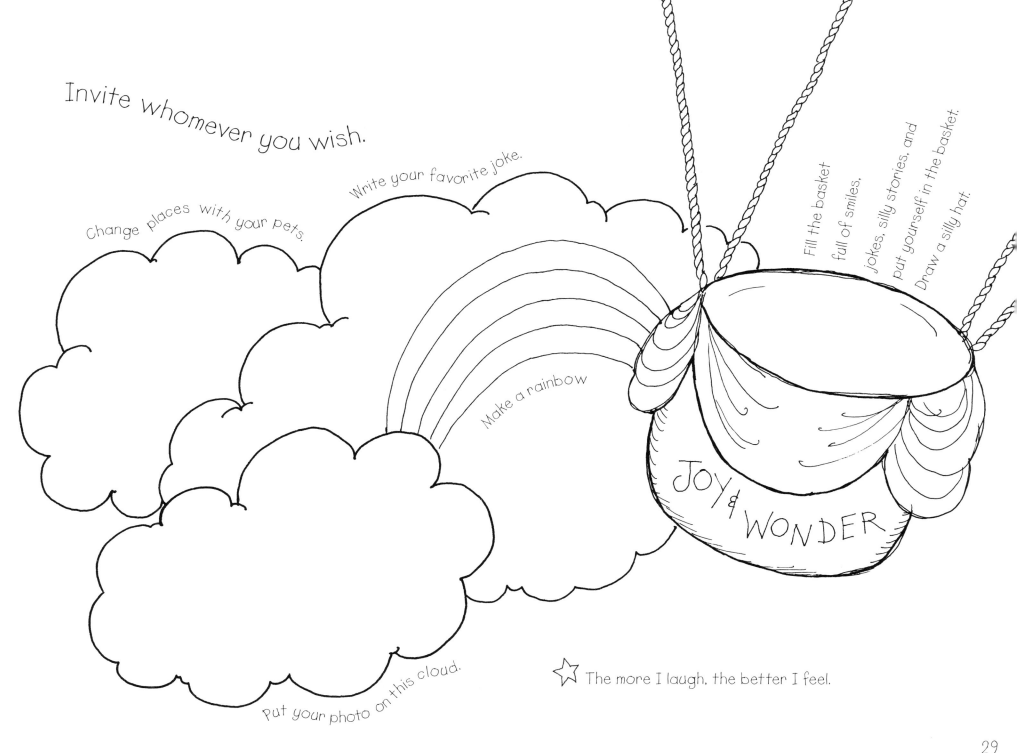

Invite whomever you wish.

Change places with your pets.

Write your favorite joke.

Make a rainbow

Put your photo on this cloud.

Fill the basket full of smiles. Jokes, silly stories, and put yourself in the basket. Draw a silly hat.

JOY & WONDER

☆ The more I laugh, the better I feel.

When you are
feeling alone and unloved,
climb into the Love Balloon.
This basket is filled with hearts.
Close your eyes and think of all the
people you could send love to.
If you need help, call on the messenger
birds that live on the nearby cloud,
Soon, the love you send out will
come back to you.
The Love Balloon is for miracles.

Write your name on a heart and send yourself love.

☆ I am a beautiful, special person.
There is no one in the world like me.
I give myself a hug.

MIRACLES

31

Write the names of people you want to send love to on the hearts.

You can visit
the Moon Balloon
anytime you like
and go anywhere you like.

Just close your eyes
and use your imagination.

It is the most powerful
magic you have.

33

The Moon Balloon
will be here,
waiting to take you
on a journey.

35

WHERE WE'VE BEEN

Less than a week from the day *The Moon Balloon* was published, a tragedy occurred in the small town of Dunblane, Scotland, when sixteen kindergarten children and their teacher were shot and killed. 725 Moon Balloon books were airlifted overseas courtesy of British Airways, and there was an outpouring of love and concern from individuals and corporate donors. *The Moon Balloon* served as a small resource in helping the survivors cope with that appalling disaster. Since Dunblane, the Moon Balloon has been used to help children in crisis in hospitals, hospices, schools and social service agencies. The book also helped numerous families who were directly involved with the tragedy of 9-11.

Joan Drescher has been doing groundbreaking work with healthcare staff and patients at MassGeneral Hospital *for* Children (MGHfC) in Boston since the fall of 2000. As Artist-in-Residence at MGHfC, she visits children's bed-sides with her "Imagination Kart" filled with art supplies, inspiring children to create their own beauty and magic. The concept for the Artist-in-Residence program is based on *The Moon Balloon* book and workshops. This book's unique layout has a focus that involves everyone in the healing process, creating community through shared experience. Joan helps children create stories and drawings that transform their hospital visit. She also presents workshops and trainings for doctors and hospital staff, enabling them to integrate the arts into medicine. For the last five years the AIR program has been funded by The Elizabeth Whiteside Charitable Foundation and The MassGeneral Hospital Ladies' Visiting Committee.

Thanks to the wonderful friendship of Dr. Tina Annoni, the Moon Balloon traveled with Joan to the Gaslini Hospital for Children in Genoa, Italy. Joan has offered numerous workshops and presentations for caregivers and children, with the support of A.M.R.I. (Associazione per le Malattie Reumatiche Infantili). Not only does the Moon Balloon decorate the hospital walls, but the staff also use it to communicate with their patients. Many Italian children contribute Moon Balloon drawings about their feelings for the hospital website. "The Friendship Balloon" was created to bridge between healthcare professionals and pediatric patients at MGHfC and A.M.R.I. at Gaslini. It is a pen pal network for children to share pictures, stories and letters. Riding on small balloons are photos of each child, with the addresses and emails of both hospitals. The healthcare professionals exchanged information and ideas, resulting in a photo book and a video. Due to the success of "The Friendship Balloon," we realized the potential for such a program to be spread all across the world.

Patients at MassGeneral Hospital for Children, Boston, MA.

WHERE WE'RE GOING

The Moon Balloon book has inspired us to create a non-profit organization called The Moon Balloon Project Inc: Building Healing Bridges for Children Through the Arts in Medicine. The Project demonstrates the valuable roles that art can play with children and families experiencing crisis, illness and loss. The Project's primary activities are: Moon Balloon workshops for children; trainings for healthcare professionals and caregivers; and the distribution of Moon Balloon books, training guides and other materials. The Project's secondary activities are to educate the public. This is accomplished through traveling exhibits, events and collaborations with colleges, hospitals, hospices and other non-profit organizations such as museums and schools. Our vision is to empower children to practice emotional literacy. The Project provides resources to families, educators and healthcare professionals. So many families have found that this book helps them to express feelings honestly and openly. *The Moon Balloon* book is used by hospitalized children in New England, the US, and internationally.

Children in crisis can experience validation and hope by communicating their feelings with others. Because we have heard from thousands of people who have loved *The Moon Balloon*, we plan to create:

- A user's guide, with chapters written by experts in the field.
- Workshops tailored to the specific needs of diverse audiences.

With stresses mounting, the pressing challenge is how to get these tools to families who need them. We would love to hear from you! Please send us your stories, comments and questions at www.themoonballoon.com. As we believe in the power of art to heal, we know this balloon will go even higher with your help!

"The Moon Balloon is a magical tool that makes our emotions fly and it colors our dreams with grace and poetry. Really, it is a wonderful gift."
   —Dr. Tina Annoni, Psychologist, Expressive Dance Therapist,
   Mente Corpo Education, Varazze, Italy

Annie Lartigau and her granddaughter, Anna Schloeder, enjoy The Moon Balloon in Quinson, France.
Drawings by the children at the Gaslini Hospital in Genoa, Italy.

THE MOON BALLOON PROJECT, A HEALING RESOURCE

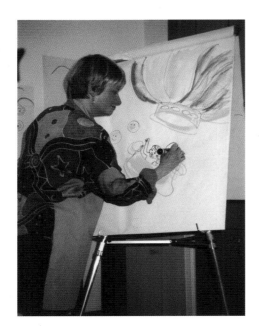

The Moon Balloon Project Inc; Building Healing Bridges for Children Through the Arts in Medicine is a 501(c)3 nonprofit organization that inspires children to express their emotions honestly and openly through playful hot air balloon symbols. It provides a safe environment enabling children and families to communicate in stressful situations. Research has shown that making art nourishes the spirit and helps the healing process of both body and mind in children. Our goals are to foster emotional literacy in all children, especially children who are ill, in transition or experiencing loss and to nurture creative connections between caregivers, educators, parents and children in America and around the world.

Training for Adults

The Moon Balloon Training is a tool for parents, teachers, healthcare professionals and all those concerned with bringing emotional healing to children. The training teaches you to provide a safe, supportive outlet to help your children cope with the stress that often accompanies everyday problems of living as well as life changing experiences such as death, illness and divorce.

- Learn how to use positive images as tools for opening the heart and creating safe environments
- Discover how symbols are used to express feelings too difficult for words
- Empower yourself and others; Let go of worry and fear, launch dreams and wishes

The training also includes an activity guide and resources for using the book in specific contexts. The contexts include: elementary school teaching, nursing, social work, child-life, medical school teaching, hospice work, chaplaincy, family therapy, and family life. This training, when given in tandem with hospitals or schools, can earn medical or educational professional credit hours. For information on upcoming workshops or training, visit our website, www.themoonballoon.com.

Workshops for Children

The Moon Balloon Workshop is a way for children to express feelings through writing, drawing, and symbols. This joyful workshop nurtures self esteem and helps children to celebrate who they are. On-the spot interactive drawings are created to help children communicate and to tell the story of the Moon Balloon. Encouraging creativity and community, children and families are encouraged to write their wishes and worries on balloons and let the balloons go into the sky.

Jaden and Alex Ackerman writing wishes and worries on their balloons.

JOIN US! THERE ARE LOTS OF WAYS TO GET INVOLVED!

- Find out how a Moon Balloon Fundraiser can raise money for your organization.
- Buy *The Moon Balloon* for your school or hospital.
- Help get *The Moon Balloon* to the greatest number of children in need through our sponsorship program. You may donate *The Moon Balloon* books, training, and workshops to your local hospital, school, hospice, family center or clinic.

Forthcoming Moon Balloon Resources include: An instruction and activity guide for caregivers that is tailored to specific disciplines and an interactive CD-Rom for caregivers and children. Please see our website for more details: **www.themoonballoonproject.org**

A healing resource for adults and adolescents:

On Wings of Light
Finding Hope When the Heart Needs Healing
Created by Joan Borysenko, Ph.D. and Joan Drescher
$16.00 USA

"This magical book of hope and spirit will comfort, heal and inspire you. It is meant to be read again and again, its wise words and uplifting images will reconnect you to who you truly are."
— Joan Klagsbrun, Ph.D., Psychologist and Director of the Wellspring Center

Donate online: **www.themoonballoonproject.org**
Donate by phone: 781-749-5179
Donate by mail: Please make check payable to The Moon Balloon Project and send to address below.

For more information about volume discounts, our sponsorship program, or to order more books, visit our website or write to:

The Moon Balloon Project, Inc.
23 Cedar Street
Hingham, MA 02043

ABOUT THE AUTHOR

Joan Drescher's pioneering work using art to mend body, mind and spirit has been recognized internationally. Her murals are found in major hospitals and health care facilities throughout the US and Canada. She is the author/illustrator of 25 children's books and a new inspirational book, *On Wings of Light—Finding Hope When the Heart Needs Healing*, co-authored with Dr Joan Borysenko. Joan is the Artist-In-Residence at MassGeneral Hospital *for* Children (MGH*f*C) in Boston, Massachusetts. She is the director of the Moon Balloon Project, Inc.: Building Healing Bridges for Children Through the Arts in Medicine. She is on the board of the Society for Arts in Healthcare and is also a fellow at the Institute for Body Mind and Spirituality at Lesley University in Cambridge, Massachusetts. She is the Artistic Director of the Institute for Interspiritual Inquiry in Boulder, Colorado.

Photo by Bob Schlowsky

the balloons go. Spirits soar as we watch them drift high into the sky. There is a real feeling of release, empowerment and community.

While working with children as the Artist in Residence at Boston's MassGeneral Hospital *for* Children, I experience on a daily basis how color and images help young patients communicate from a place far deeper than words. Some patients actually require less pain medication while creating art. Many children receiving chemotherapy are overwhelmed by powerful emotions. To help empower them during treatment, they fill moon balloon baskets with images and words, symbolically releasing their emotions. While presenting workshops for children and caregivers in Europe, I found *The Moon Balloon* transcended all language barriers. The same emotions: anger, sadness, worry and joy, were understood through the balloon symbols and friendship became our universal language.

Author's Note:

It has been a gift for me to hear the stories and insights this book has created for children and caregivers. Each story has been like a bright star shining though the dark night sky. It is so important in today's troubled world to tell the stories of hope and discovery and to allow children to express feelings honestly and openly.

In my workshops, children and caregivers write wishes with magic markers on yellow helium balloons and worries on blue ones. We form a large circle and each child is given the opportunity to tell the group what their worries are. Even the smallest children can draw a symbol of what's been bothering them. Wishes often start at the personal level and expand into universal visions for world peace. We all hold hands, count to ten and let

Today's children are under more pressure and schedules than ever before. They are also exposed to media that features violence and excess consumption. The new stress balloon has a basket to help children identify and record their everyday worries and stresses. During a workshop for 4th graders, a small boy said to me, "Make sure you draw a big clock with feet, because time always runs away from me." After the stress balloon, the peace balloon provides a safe and welcoming place for children to go just to be themselves. No matter who the audience, these symbolic balloons have helped children and adults to communicate, opening hearts to hope and healing. It is because of you that I am republishing this book. Please keep sending stories and quotes as you ride in the Moon Balloon and continue the journey of the human spirit.